This Hole Called January

This Hole Called January

Paula Jane Remlinger

thistledown press

Thistledown Press Ltd.
410 2nd Ave. North
Saskatoon, Saskatchewan, S7K 2C3
www.thistledownpress.com

Library and Archives Canada Cataloguing in Publication

Title: This hole called January / Paula Jane Remlinger.
Names: Remlinger, Paula Jane, 1971- author.
Description: Poems.
Identifiers: Canadiana 20190063211 | ISBN 9781771871938 (softcover)
Classification: LCC PS8635.E4955 T55 2019 | DDC C811/.6—dc23

Cover and book design by Jackie Forrie
Author photo by Jane Isinger
Printed and bound in Canada

Canada Council for the Arts	Conseil des Arts du Canada

Thistledown Press gratefully acknowledges the financial support of the Canada Council for the Arts, the Saskatchewan Arts Board, and the Government of Canada for its publishing program.

Contents

7 Origins

8 Burnt Sienna

9 Finnegan's Wake

10 Bringing Down the House

11 At the Crossroads

12 Gardening for Fun and Relaxation

13 Devil's Leather

14 At the Sundown Drive-In

15 Gazebra

16 Crow

18 A Crueller Trap

19 Life and Death of the Richardson's Ground Squirrel

20 Mind the Dark

21 In Every Story There's a Wolf

23 On His Workbench

24 The Weight of Words

25 Stoop, 6:30 pm, a Monday in September

26 An Elk in Waskesiu

27 No Stomach for Prophecy

28 I Hope You Understand

29 You Drift Away on a Thinning Breeze

31 Old Man Winter 1

32 This Hole Called January

33 The Girl Who Dances with Bears

34 Glory Be

35 Oranges

36 in the days before your death, you fed us

37 Winter Sill

38 Phases

39 Ode to Horace (in the Freezer Awaiting Burial)

40 Auroras

41 Salty Dog

42 Lavalife

43 This Is for the Neighbour's Cat

44 James Bond Considers Retirement

45 What to Expect When You're Not Expecting

46 Sole Survivor

48 Suicide Loop

49 The Arsonist

50 Artifice

55 If I Die, Blame the Movies

56 The Girl Who Drew Lines on her Skin

57 The Superman Poems

63 Girls Named Paula

Origins

after John Minczeski

My name a lost folk tale, night caravan,
remembers nothing of its birth,
the Romani syllables, their shape and breath.

Abandoned on a doorstep, my name swaddled
in rags, a gold coin marooned in its tiny fist.
A mother carried it, squalling, inside to warm
and solid German ways, nursed it on sheep's milk.
A father fed it brown bread, potatoes, tea-steeped
discipline and newsprint. It grew up

never knowing truth. My name caught a freighter
west to Canada, counted wife, child, and goat
as wealth. It learned coyote. The cruelty of snow. Became
a furrow shadowing the plough, turned unbroken hills
to fields, buried seeds and sons. Heard wheat jangling,
a thousand golden tambourines.

Burnt Sienna

before we learned flesh should not be
turquoise, brick, or lemon;

before thick black lines
divined paths for us to follow;

before Prussian Blue had to duck
and cover beneath our desks;

before Indian Red faded like Indian summer,
and the world became ultra,
electric, neon, atomic —

it was the colour
of cinnamon toast and foxes,
dirty pennies and rusty bottlecaps,
leaves crumpled under new shoes,
bottle-brush tails of squirrels.

we buried gold on burnt sienna shores,
coloured mountains on Mars,
drew spiny-backed dinosaurs in Mesozoic swamps
until the bells and shouts of recess
called us away.

"Burnt Sienna" was one of the colours being considered for retirement by Crayola Crayons in 2003.

Finnegan's Wake

Mr. Dress-up wore the sad clown make-up,
hobo whiteface complete with tear. Bowler,

black and round as Finnegan's still staring eyes,
flower cocked in its crown. Daisies were his favourite.

The Tickle-Trunk refused to open, latch rusted shut,
its brassy smile turned upside-down. Finally, coaxed

with oil and crowbar, it released its mourning:
top hat, sailor's jacket, a trench coat pale

as grief. Casey had been crushed
by the Treehouse toppled in a storm,

didn't live to see the pup, flat and empty
in his shoebox — he looks so natural,

like the victim of some degenerative wasting
disease — children growing older, believing

in less. Finnegan's head ruffled by plastic hands,
the perfect dog who never barked,

the too-many-times-through-the-wash scruffiness,
his fur grey as television's first breath.

Bringing Down the House

No one is surprised when the storm begins, sky stippled
with rain-dark clouds, and soon lightning begets thunder
begets a deluge worthy of the Scottish play droning
under the red-and-white curves of the tent, flaps barely
holding. The wind slaps us like a lady scorned. Players
shout to be heard, Macbeth bombastic in his confidence,

and his bride smiles, encourages murder, pokes holes
in his pride with imaginary daggers. On the riverbank,
in latent summer heat, the tent blows down in the driving
rain, flood worthy of the Old Testament, and actors scatter,
their stage unroofed, the whole mess dank and dirty,
a foundling circus, arms outstretched to beg for more,

another minute, a reprieve for ill-made choices. I could not
simply leave. Shakespeare corrupted our language, gave us
thees and thous, so I absquatulated. Copacetic for once
with the misery of August weather. In the flash, you and I
hold hands in the black and silver rain, the faintest glint of smiles.

We are a daguerreotype.

At the Crossroads

The rumours have always been there, flying like flags.

Not his real father. Mother got knocked up by a stranger
named Gabe. Can't really blame her. He looked like an angel.

Women gather at the well, whisper about the holy
spirit moving in them too. Laughter sputters.

My folks don't talk about it much. Dad keeps
to himself, spends his time turning wood, calloused hands

smoothing the curved lip of cup and bowl, gentle turn
of a walking stick. Mother's on her knees in the temple every day.

I'm just a regular guy whose parents think he walks on water.
Meant for greatness. Chosen one. Son of God. Saviour.

But sand still scratches when it steals inside my sandals, wind
tears my robe. No angels appear when children throw names.

Bastard. Blasphemer. No one to purge my dreams
of bloodied babes as Herod hunts the child who would be King.

All I want is a girl's warm mouth muscling over my body, small
breasts held to my lips, my arms snaking around her desert skin.

A moment when I am no one's son or saviour. Flesh and blood.
The holy ghost shooting through me like stars.

Gardening for Fun and Relaxation

You maintain a tidy prison. Irises
in upright rows, pansies raise pinched faces.
Carrots and radishes, green tops waving,
the sharp-bladed salute of onions and herbs —

I plant a poison garden: hemlock, nightshade,
wolfsbane, monkshood. Let the earth bloom
thistle, the snapping calamity of dragons, bleeding
hearts, impatiens, rue, nettles to swarm the ground,
their black-tipped thorns a warning.

You offer me pansies. When I was a child,
I plucked their petals like wings.

Devil's Leather

Church basement, Saturday night. Jesus,
butterfly-watchful, pinned between flag
and Queen. Squares on paper plates, punch-
heavy cups, and the one-two tap of anxious

pairs. Lines of opposing armies
separated by rulers — one foot
the measure of innocence. Mary Janes
to the left, White Bucks on the right.

Shoes shuffle and scuff, trumpet tussles
with drum, clarinet croons a call to swing.
Reflections wink from the devil's leather,
buffed to coax stars in a black patent sky.

White picket fancies, small pink bows,
silk and cotton. First shades of longing
flash quick as creation. Hands bridge
the divide, Michelangelo's Adam

reaching, first boy, first girl, first
urge to touch, uncharted
universe, a rising skirt unfurls,
milky way twirling at the centre.

At the Sundown Drive-In

Strawberry whirl lip gloss, candy-floss cheeks,
big-splash lashes and his buttered hands, slick

lips shiny with oil and salt. Her
bubblegum snap drowns a hundred flirting horns

under muscle-car tires; in the back
of the ancient Eldorado, a leather and metal mattress,

she can smell her own damp heat, the late pollen bloom,
back-road bonfires she's not supposed to know. Beer sits

on the palate like a flat stone. At home, mother watches
the ghost moths stuttering, reckless against the yellow light.

She'll wait a little longer.

Gazebra

I stumble home drunk. Under the gazebo's peak, my smoke coils,
my head stone-heavy, body stretched between two chairs,
then, soft breeze through grass, crickets, the hard clump of
hooves.
Hooves. Zebra eyes meet mine. Her stripes less black,
less white, less stark, more lightning and thunder merged. I long
to carve a new language. Unperturbed, she gazes at me.

We dream of long prairie grasses, of steppe, savannah,
the slough where water buffalo slump and lions sleep. Birds
whirl overhead, beaks the colour of pearl; trees unfurl
the elephant sound of morning.

Prairie is the word my tongue forgets.

Crow

Words are dark rainbows
without roots, a murder of crows
— Patrick Lane, "A Murder of Crows"

i.

It is night. The moon is a shell
tossed on black sand,
edge scalloped by clouds.

In each of us there is a death —
the heart consumed still
beating, plucked from
a cage of bone.

ii.

I found it hiding in the grass beside the gravel road:
a discarded blackness, which from a distance could have been
a forgotten winter toque, or a tire snapped like licorice.
A crow fallen from its spring nest,
old pine's dark and thorny crown.

I ran for father, bent low
over new seed laid in damp earth.
The rough blue of work-shirt as I tugged,
my eyes big as rain-clouds, his face lost
behind the soiled red handkerchief;
he closed his tanned hand over mine, small as an egg,
let himself be led through uncut grass, drowsing
dandelions, under the broken limbs of pines.

We knelt, air bright with crushed clover,
parted the green, breeze lifting
the untried wings, small fierce beak snapping

at father's fingers as if they were worms.
Crow, a wooden hammer thrumming
against his hands as he lifted,
its voice scraping my ears
the long lean strop of a blade on leather.

iii.

The way a dog leans into scent, I follow my father,
the still body still warm, the dark crumpled wings,
unseeing eyes. We bury it behind the whirling pinwheels,
beak reaching down for the fresh green shoots.

The wind cools my bare arms as I run home, hand
slipping from my father's, distance sprouting
between us like weeds. The dark eyes of crows
in the splintering sun watch the door close.

iv.

It is night. Still.
Words find roots
burrowing through cool earth,
the bones of birds. The heart
a strawberry stone, waiting
for a clover spring.
The crows' return.
A father's hand.

A Crueller Trap

Mice spill from drywall holes,
from pink insulation; black-eyed,
furtive, they inhabit limbo, peripheral
vision. The skiff of claws on concrete.

We wage a winter campaign. We set
peanut butter traps, cheddar, a double
cream brie. They lick wires bare, feast
but never spring the catch.

Yet empty wine bottles hold mice, bent
as in the womb. We have to break
the necks to spill the dead, and yes

I wanted them dead, but not this incremental
shrivelling, hunger gnawing its nest.

Life and Death of the Richardson's Ground Squirrel

name too long for a proper warning
Gopher, gopher! swerves
the car, but not in time

brome grass sweeps small brown
death aside, a punk rock thistle-top
bows its crown in mourning

Mind the Dark

there, in the corner, the sharpening
of knives. flame-spurs drop where
metal grinds steel against stone.

they're coming for me
on rubber-soled shoes,
carrying icepicks casual
as pens, Shröedinger's marionettes

unstrung. thoughts creep, belly low, quiet
as fog on gravel. I demand they turn
their sockets out. emptied of eyes, there's
lint, tissues, ink spots black as tacks.

In Every Story There's a Wolf

Girl. Hood. Basket. Woods. We are
meant to listen to our mothers.

Woodcutter wields his axe, measures worth
in concentric rings, the honed edge of a blade.
He lumbers, trailing splinters like breadcrumbs
down darkening turns.

Do not stray. Follow the way
like a lolling tongue.

Grandmother, lost in quilted sleep, deep
as a pond, hands gnarled, voice a twilight
croak, its timbres reed and bullfrog, waits
for the splay of red.

The house is a safe. Closed and locked,
the door. It is protected. Probably.

Woodcutter drips sap from his moon-glint axe,
drags trunk and severed limbs to the growing pile.
The expected hero cuts down the forest, arrives
too late for supper, his edge grown dull.

Girl is the sweetest hunger. New, red-ribboned.
Girl rides the blush, curls inward, a rosebud. Abed.

Wolf knows shadows, wears night.
He is the thief of hearts, eats each
with practised ease, chews the challenge
of old bones. His smile is toothpick-clean.

How big your eyes, your ears, your teeth.
There are versions of every truth.

Wolf's jaws close the trap, but Grandmother
and Girl hold hands in the dark cramp of Wolf's belly,
remake their tomb a womb, and Wolf gives birth
to the red-hooded child, grandmother bones.

Villagers sew rocks inside, stitch his wound
with sinew thread, a woodsman's knot. Tag
his crime in rickrack tracks, leave him for dead.

On His Workbench

Crescent wrench, a weight in my hand.
Five months it lies, unobtrusive, dust
drawn magnetically like filings. Its angles
and curves clearer than any photograph

of you. Everything here is unfinished. A ship
without a bottle, rigging hopelessly tangled. The dollhouse
door that creaked. My first bike. The casual wrench
promises your return, a bookmark, but the air is stagnant.

Time, empty vessel in a blown-glass sea, waiting
to buckle, splinter. The captain's daughter is tied
to the mainsail, tears scarring her cheeks. Her survival
is inevitable.

The garage smells of wood chips and damp, a cemetery
chill, moist breath of paint, oil, modeller's glue. Heart,
a nervous drummer, rolling tympani, the tsunami crash.
Wrench in hand, I think of wood and it bruises;

imagine crescent moons and my palms ache.
Blue as old glass, a beetle scrabbles away.
Chitinous thorax cracks like a walnut, the wrench
stained. It fails to satisfy.

The Weight of Words

A moth, artful shadow on the library wall,
clinging to paper roses, pale leaves, settles
on my desk, wings delicate grey, soft as a wasp nest.

I strike it
with the authoritative
Oxford Canadian Edition, hardcover.
17,000 new entries, full pronunciations, and encyclopedia
section. Smash three sets of legs, a thorax,
compound eyes, abdomen, proboscis, antennae

with the most useful, practical, and informative
dictionary available.

Stoop, 6:30 PM, a Monday in September

You're not home.

I suspected you wouldn't be, but I came anyway.
Not sure what that says about me. Possibility
of company was good, but so's this.
Your neighbours are prairie-dog curious,
but no one questions my right to this space.

Two guys in sweat-drenched tees wrestle
the ugliest brown couch I've ever seen
over the ground floor suite's railing. Its stout
legs refuse to move, until it's heave-ho, over
she goes, like an elephant climbing a mountain.

I hear the hiss-pop beer tops, the aluminium clink.
The couch cowboys congratulate themselves
behind sliding doors. There is only me

and the empty lot. Worn jean jacket, my good black
pants dusty. Autumn cement, a ground-out cigarette, air
wafting boiled beans, curry, something satisfying I cannot name.

An Elk in Waskesiu

Chocolate ruff edges the almond hide.
His flanks are hard with muscle, and the earth
resounds every step. His rack branches, tangles
with the failing sun as though to dislodge it
from the horizon. He skirts the drift of snow geese
bedded in bowls of cool sand.

I'm not quite a safe distance behind. Knee-deep
in evening, he dips his grand candelabra to lap
the lake's edge. It glistens, lit with the last
pale light. He drinks his fill.
                    The shutter snaps.

He becomes the trees, violet dusk on haunch and rump. Antlers
now poplar, white birch, his breath the fog. Diminishing.

No Stomach for Prophecy

Inside sleek ribs, I winter,
trapped. Fingernails scratch
Jonah was here —
three days and nights all I can
stomach. The stars, distant
memory. Sun, a splint of light
between baleen.

This is the whale's dark belly,
perpetual night. An ocean
creeps around me, blind
fish feed on silence, on cold.

I Hope You Understand

They tell me the grave is lovely. Your name
incised in granite, grey as the elephant sky that stood
vigil when we laid you there. The grass trim,
and a vase built in for flowers. You would've appreciated
the care taken by the carver, the gardener.

I haven't returned. I believe their reports.
I've become the prodigal daughter, a wayward kite
unspooled. The tug is constant. But you never liked
cemeteries either, wouldn't blame me.

Most days, your loss skirts the back lot of thought, indistinct
from this business of living. Not remembered, simply known.

You Drift Away on a Thinning Breeze

(for Susan W.)

i.

Your hair was your best feature. The way it swept
your shoulders like a golden cape, matching the sway
of hips, catching light, men's eyes. We laughed because
once you made it to the salon, saw the moult of hair against
unswept tile, saw the flash and snip of hummingbird
scissors, and ran, blonde waves coursing behind you.

ii.

I touch the smooth bowl of your head. New growth begins
slowly, a prickle of seedlings seeking the sun you once carried

on your back. Even soft cloth is strong enough to raise redness
like a mouth. Your skin, now a warren of bed sores, welts.

There is no comfort in these sheets. Body, bent and sharp
as peaks, a frame stretched too thin. Your cheeks have eroded.

Shadows lie in hollows, veins ink your skin, translucent
as vellum. You are smaller than before, though your bones
displace flesh, seem larger. Awkward as a teenager, you shed

another self, become smaller
and whiter every moment,
curling toward
centre.

iii.

We used to play with paper dolls, punch out their bodies from
our mothers' magazines, dress the girls who floated on air.

Now you can slip through walls, waft away on a breeze, slide
under doors. Clothes hang too heavy, enough to bury you.

Even in a paper gown, you drown. I watch you retreat beneath
sterile sheets, seeking silence. My mouth is an open well.
Wishes tumble backwards, swallowed, anticipating

your absence.

Old Man Winter 1

Old man winter's got a gap-toothed scowl on his stubbled
crag. He spits blizzards like Copenhagen chew, expectorates
Nor'easters in autumn's brass spittoon.

Summer's child isn't welcome here. These river bones ache,
a prehistoric fang embedded in the meat of me. I'm cold-packed
and hung. Whaler's hook jailed. A seasoning of snow.

This Hole Called January

There's a man dead in the corner. The bear wears
his skin for warmth, unwinds it like a peel.

We live with what consumes us. Bear licks blunt
claws, gouges trench the walls. Winter days lie

dormant, a woollen itch that can't be soothed or stopped.
Drowsing in frigid anaesthetic, sixty degrees from summer,

Bear gives a heated growl. He blinks, slow
as melt, hunger unappeased.

The Girl Who Dances with Bears

Bear is leashed to a rusted chain. Winter exhales
Shostakovich and carnival paint while bear wears stiff-collared
shame, ridiculous knit hat, pom-poms dangling. He is a hunger
cave, an empty sack, clawing days into memory. We believe
it's possible to tame the wild. The chain is important, the break
inevitable. Each link a mile to keep us
apart, every muscular pull a revolver, its single bullet
spinning like a Ferris wheel. Remember the animal. His keeper
wears a cross-stitch face, lips lopsided as a circus tent.
The bearded lady strokes bear. Look how safe.

Closer, he calls, *my darlings. For you alone.*

Ursa Major, the great bear dances. Star skeleton
with limbs flung wide. Asterism of cup and handle
to dip, to drink from the well of sky. Let us watch.
I would grow fur like Callisto, let myself be hunted to feel
earth beneath rough pads, lay teeth to salmon scales, skim
twigs like warm kabobs. Today, I wish to be a girl again, see
the towering beast with his shag, paws big as my head. I would
burrow my face in his blood-thatched pelt, wear him
like a coat, tuck into arms meant to crush. Feel him skin
back the worst of me, root out the berry heart.

Glory Be

The mole maintains the path to Hell. A bargain struck
in Eden's shade, soft hiss of serpent's tongue, and he,
brown spot against a cabbage leaf, shrewd
eyes not blind as belief, over
looked by everyone, forgotten in the green

almost. Mole mines a slow spiral
down, remakes a path old as sin. Ring twists
upon ring, a gyroscope fixed at the centre. He
shovels wet earth, worm and grub. Sprawled,
belly dirt-hard, he feeds on the black, appetite
insatiable, and opens veins wide enough
for a soul to slip, swallowed

like a goldfish — surfacing
where air is fire, water burns blue, a current
of cinders fingers the river banks. Souls emerge,
grey, heavy, malleable as lead, laconic
victims of consequence. No room for questions

buried this deep. Old souls eschew the new,
keep silent, knowing time as it was beginning,
now, world without end.

Oranges

Mid-winter, small town Saskatchewan
and the Co-op stocks nothing but
oranges, apples, bananas, more oranges.

I've eaten so many I'm turning bright as Jupiter,
heavy with pulp and juice. No chance of scurvy.
I smell of Florida, old wood floors waxed by widows
at St. Stephen's. I will be stuffed in a Christmas stocking,
toe nestled with almonds, a handful of sweets.

You can open me.

The perfect curvature. Inhale
my heady sweetness, cloves and oranges.

in the days before your death, you fed us

(for Susan W.)

Alberta beef, rare, bloody; bison with pink
cracked peppercorns, their fire-bang whiff of cap guns
and smoke; oven-warm buns, fat as winter mitts;
white asparagus fingers; grilled peppers, cross-hatched;
mushrooms broiled in garlic, basil, capers.

The meal is luxury, a restaurant feast we could never afford, but
you are 31 and thin as a plate. You give us a table to bear the load,
distract us from your brittle spine, the hum-pump of the oxygen
tank, heartbeat-regular, quiet as background music.

You laugh and kiss my cheek, the faintest brush
of chocolate, sticky raspberry lips, and this is the last time
I will see your sweetness, your smile. I leave with a tinfoil
swan, its neck bowed, leftovers spilling from the seams.

Winter Sill

An ice-locked edge I'm forced to pry
to steal a pendulum's breath.

Summer flies crust old paint flakes,
legs stiff, wings a lead-veined wax.

They line the sill, blue-bottles antique
with dust. Small summer ghosts.

Scrape them off, watch them
spiral,

vanish —
black eyes, pocking the snow.

Phases

i.

A trickster steals from night's
table, leaving scattered grains
of salt, darkness. The china plate
wheels off the edge, escapes
into wedges, a serving of cheese.

ii.

The peppermint hangs frost
inside my mouth. I weary of its taste
through a month of empty nights.
A host, a hollow, a slow-draining
halo, a sinkhole for dreams.

See it there? A wafer, a dog's smile,
an ocean-going skull, cream
for feral cats, saucer tipped.

It is the blind eye of time.
Creep softly. Make no sound.
Let the world turn and turn
in its fragile light.

Ode to Horace (in the Freezer Awaiting Burial)

One small dead goldfish
beside frozen corn and a gallon
bucket of Co-op Neapolitan ice-cream.

He would've liked the tricolour wave
though he knew only a turquoise-pebbled
aquarium's roiling froth of oxygen, a plastic
castle, manna rained from gods above.

I was outvoted, everyone against
the porcelain express, the filtration plant
not a fit end for family.

So he keeps inside a Ziploc coffin, grows milky
crystals on stiff fins. Spring is coming.

Auroras

The dishwasher whirs, pans soak in the sink.
Silence impossible, inside or out. Appliances
hum. Even the sleeping cat purrs.

Television muted blue-white, the northern sky is green as
ghost-light, mirrored in the clean snow. Light folds itself like sheets
on a clothesline. They say you can hear them sing: static

electric, bottled lightning. Overhead a satellite's white eye
blinks. How small this world, how like a pyrite vein
in gold-panned rock this moment gleams.

Wait for the shiver — the dead have things to say before they rest.
Pines speak. The wind, an owl's wing. The clear ping of icicles
plummeting. Night umbrellas us — seven billion carbon

specks on a whirling globe. We stencil our names in the stars,
connect the dots in bull and swan, crab and archer. A time-lapsed
photograph. We move too fast. You reach for me, glove-handed.

We barely know each other through winter layers. Beneath
the wheeling heavens, you kiss me; the world drops away.
Soundless, we spin and spin.

Salty Dog

Somewhere a bar extant in my mind, home
of the perfect Salty Dog:

1½ ounces gin
5 ounces grapefruit

squeezed by hand, pulp pressed on pinwheel ridges, the yellow
plastic juicer just like my mother's. Tupperware, 1964. Hi-ball
glass, salt-collared cobalt, hard square kernels like a Riopelle
painting, laid with brush and trowel.

First sip, a gritty tickle. Bombay Sapphire slugs
in citrus trails thick with salt, the after-burn
of bad ideas. Juniper, blue on my tongue, four-hundred-
year history swallowed, absorbed, belched back. Howl.

Lavalife

His online shot is smoking, dreadlocks braided black,
hot enough to drench your wettest dreams. You sizzle,

water on a forge. He likes Latin dance, Moruga Scorpion
cliff-diving his senses, occasional ritual sacrifice. Calls

himself "magma-nanimous." He's thermonuclear, a squeeze
with bedrock promises, a'a melting to uh-huh, and you'll ignore

faults, evidence of craters. Heart tremors. Burn. No one's perfect.
Too bad up close he's a half-baked potato, head adrift

in self-sustaining vog, heavy as pot haze. Anger management's
not his forté, vents steaming, and you should've known

volcanoes make bad blind dates. But next month, on time
as tribute, you'll be back. An unlit fuse looking for a match.

This Is for the Neighbour's Cat

A black-and-white scrapper brings the fight
to my yard. Fifteen pounds of cat-scratch
fever drums a challenge onto paw-printed glass.

Three times my kitten's size, he bullies reflections,
hiss-scowls and sputters, yowls at the windows,
fangs bared. His claws leave ragged screens.

He pees on my lilacs, rosebush, marks territory,
his male prerogative to spray wherever
he likes, ass-backward stream of holy yellow stink.

He unearths my bulbs, vomits chewed grass,
half-shrews, then climbs the cedar fence, saunters
its tightrope length, achieves the shed's pitched roof

and perches, a useless weather-vane, indicating
no direction — just menace, dander, and piss.

James Bond Considers Retirement

"I'll buy you a delicatessen."
— Ernst Blofeld, villain, *For Your Eyes Only* (1981)

For a moment Bond trades the trench coat
for an apron ripe with salami spice, mustard
stretched thin as winter sun, the everyday clatter,
and thinks of kissing Moneypenny —
smoked ham wants a hint of Dijon — and wonders
what it would be like to stop minding

his Ms and Qs, pens that shoot
but don't write, women and cars
likely to blow without warning. It hurts
these days to slalom, leap from a plane,
wrestle sharks or swarthy men. It's harder
to make love underwater, needing
the oxygen tank more often than not,
harder to drink those damn martinis,
liver shrivelled like a rancid olive.

Everything's harder.
(Almost everything.)

For a moment Bond hesitates —
he hovers, then tips the chopper politely
like a gentleman's hat and you plummet,
revenge green as dill on the tip of your tongue.

What to Expect When You're Not Expecting

If you don't mind me asking
are you on The Pill, or waiting,
praying, ovulating, taking
your temperature like a good Catholic girl?

    I know a couple, a doctor, a specialist.
    A sister, daughter, a second-hand friend.

Are you worried something's wrong
with you, your eggs too old, fallopian tubes,
or with him, his sperm, his tongue-tied vasectomy,
Viagra jokes? Even gays have kids these days.

    I know a woman who had six miscarriages,
    a D&C, ectopic pregnancy, infertility treatments,
    hysterectomy,   phantom labour, non-viable
    embryo, stillbirth.

So you don't like children,
sex, you're selfish, haven't considered
your parents, options, obligations,
your responsibility, the future?

No. It simply didn't happen.
No answers exactly
right, exactly true
or mine.

Sole Survivor

So you think bartenders hear it all?
Well, let me tell ya there ain't no better way to know somebody
than to sell them shoes. Walk a mile in someone's shoes?
You don't even have to walk in 'em to know how far they've come.

The way a guy slips the heel, stepping on the back
of the leather, scuffing it like an old tire,
or a gal raises shoe to hand to slide it off
with ease. Whether the foot is small and curved
like a Roman arch, flesh smooth under stretched
nylon, the shimmer of painted toes beneath sheer taupe,
or whether it's wide and flat as a fishing barge,
a foot that's hauled a load for many a mile
down too many streams to count, blue veins
shivering through valleys of flesh, corns
and bunions festering beside outcrops of bone,
the curved knob of an arthritic toe rubbing a shine
against the soft inside of the shoe, warm and bronze
like the belly of the Buddha, I can tell ya stories.

I've spent my life on my knees on factory-issue carpets,
every day another ugly step-sister shrugging her size eleven
into a child's slipper of glass, too easily shattered.
Every day another tongue lolling from its beaten mouth.
Every pair so easily replaced by another pair,
another white box from a tower of white boxes.

They all come to me sooner or later.
Those who like leather, all straps and ties, flesh
tight as a miser's wallet, or buckles and baubles,
the glossy flash of black patent reflecting

chandelier stars. Slick and sharp compass-point
heels that pebble the path with dents, indelible.

I've been here since snake-skin boots, since Adam
and Eve. Gave Noah a deal on a gross
of rubber boots. Sold sandals to Jesus.

At the end of days, there'll be shoe prints
in the dust of the world, toe-shaped tears,
stilettos stabbing through the earth to cinders,
and I will grind what's left beneath my shattered heel.

Suicide Loop

A pinwheel, coin toss, gravity's truth.
Final soliloquy poisoning the air.
Sidewalk canvas for all a body contains.

I fill my lungs with city, let it bear me down. There are
few witnesses. Pigeons disturbed by turbulence sputter
in the choking smoke of old engines. Startled

onlookers point to the strange gaunt bird plummeting.
The office tower, a full-length mirror, captures
the willow-bend of my back, wind-flushed cheeks,

the glow of decision. For one perfect moment, I am grace.
The dream is always the same: hair, dark and tentacled.
My second-best dress. Daisy-head bent between empty hands.

The Arsonist

His hands are pitch and flint, steel
and tinder. Each finger flame-tipped.

He watches the world burn. Breathes
kerosene, lungs starved of everything
but fire, indiscriminate, glutton
for the exotic: paduak, koa, a sliver
of bloodwood, wallpaper, grandma's credenza.

IKEA offers kindling, some assembly
required. Smoke rises from the carpet, noses
corners like a blind dog. All is reduced.

The world goes deaf when windows burst,
fire-glazed glass dusts the sidewalk, barren
trees, and he is there. At the end of all things.

Artifice

1. Out of Context

"One holds the other's head in her hands
like a mirror."
— Ted Kooser, "Cosmetics Department"

How does one keep a head together?
Hat box, make-up, necklace, garrotte.
Avoid sun and the old-fashioned truth.

She arranges the head on her dresser, builds it
a foundation, cold cream and powder. Concealer.
Each passing second deadens the skin.

She pretties its face: liner, shadow, applies a gloss
of lipstick and cream rouge. Dusting of decay.
Clipped-wing lashes curl, resist the cheek's cavernous
fall, the eye's sinkhole. The smile withered in place.

2. Essentials

Oil of Olay All Day Moisture Foundation, Fair Honey (Miel Clair)
35 ml, (1.1 fl oz. liq.) Created for Normal to Dry Skin,
continuously moisturizes for 11 hours.
Trixie Belden, perpetually 14, girl detective, has a best friend
named Honey with long blonde hair, pale skin,
and clear blue eyes. Honey rides horses and lives in a mansion
on the hill. She was never happy until she met Trixie.

Sweet and golden, pure as summer, Honey
has no need for makeup. She radiates warmth
without a pimple, a period, or breasts   continuously
for thirty-four books.

Cover Girl 220, Contouring Blush (Fard Contour), Purely Plum (Prune Pure), 8 g (.29 oz.)

The product claims it produces *Instant Cheekbones*:
If I just add water, they will grow firmer,
more defined: the curve of escarpment,
white slope of bone.
Or will my skin shrink inward,
lips the silent O
of a fish mouthing at shadows?

My paternal grandmother thought my mother was an Indian
because she had high cheekbones, black hair, red lips.
No matter that her skin was Irish-pale, she was Catholic
and therefore suspicious .

Cover Girl 240, Contouring Blush (Fard Contour), Sophisticated Sable (Zibeline Sophistiquée)

Zibeline – a Parisian mistress abiding
in a sumptuous boudoir (never just a bedroom),
waiting for the heartbeat knock, the moonlit shape to slip
beneath her satin sheets, emboss her skin with kisses
stolen
from another woman's lips.

CG *Lipslicks, 4g (.14 oz.):*
006R, Hint of Mauve (Soupçon de Mauve)

Doll mouths are lipstick pink
as if natural, part of every girl's body
except they're plastic.

3078, demure (modeste)

so shy and pink, it doesn't rate a capital letter,
shrinks from harsh light, undue attention,
fades to invisible by mid-afternoon.

Bronze Goddess 2217 (Déesse du Cuivre)

What Barbie would have worn
if given a choice.

My mother's favourite lipstick is
Revlon's *Wine & Roses.*
They stopped making it
ten years ago.

She hunts for the same colour
through new bifocals, peering at varying shades.

Don't use the testers, you'll catch things, diseases, germs —
who knows where those girls' lips have been?

She suspects they've changed the name to something
she'd have to wear dark glasses and a trench coat to buy:
Amber Ablaze, Brazen Raisin, Va Va Va Bloom.

She chooses Revlon's *Wine with Everything,*
the one that matches memory,
carefully smooths it on at home, pressing her lips together,
a flower snug between parchment.
Checks the mirror, doesn't like the way it shines,
the lines around her mouth more visible, a shade   off.

She erases it with a Kleenex, red blossom
on a field of snow.

Maybelline Eyelash Curler, metal, made in the USA
(No other distinguishing features)

Archaeological Find, 2097, University of Saskatchewan, Canada, Exhibit 175A: Torture device allegedly used to pinch women's eyelashes between lightly padded metal rims, its guillotine-like parts squeezing the lash into a wave-like form considered attractive to potential sexual partners for its replication of the curve of a woman's shape. A black liquid known as "mascara" (ingredients unknown) was routinely applied to the lashes to further enhance the eyes.
There are unsubstantiated reports of such devices causing tearing and pain.

Maybelline Volum' Express Mascara WX267, Brown Black

Mine never looked like "Bette Davis eyes,"
lashes curled long and lush. How I wanted those eyes.

Revlon Coffee Bean Eyeshadow 003 (Grain de Café), 6.2 g —
Lift to read directions <<<HERE/ICI

DIRECTIONS: *For highlighting, sweep pale shadow over lid or brow bone with wide end of applicator. For defining lid, use mid-tone shadow. For greater depth of colour, slightly dampen applicator before use. Use clean fingertip to blend thoroughly.*

Repeat in French.

Cover Girl 110, Eye Enhancers (Fard Accent), 3 KT
Shimmering Sands (Sable Chatoyant)
(including:

Satin Earth - *Ocre Satiné*
Toasted Sand - *Sable Grillé*
Sunkissed Sand - *Sable du Désert)*

French for sand is *sable.*
French for sable is *zibeline.*

Trim Tweezers, metal, Bassett USA, 84

Archaeological Find, 2097, University of Saskatchewan,
Exhibit 175B:

Metal is marked by a triangular pattern,
which may represent Aboriginal feather designs.
The metalwork (clearly) is meant to assist users
in maintaining a grip on the instrument during operation.

A device used to remove body hair in a neat and
bloodless way. Thought to be preferred by women
who rebelled against the more controversial method
of depilation which involved dragging sharpened
metal blades over the skin or applying hot wax
for swift (but not pain-free) removal.

Particularly useful in combatting the dreaded
"Uni-brow." See Exhibit Catalogue, p. 28, for details.

Cornsilk Light Translucent Pressed Powder 6739-32, 0.35 oz./9.9 g

square blue case opens an oyster
revealing a mirror round and gleaming
nothing fits completely a nose a cheek
one eye
or the other a face in
pieces
one of Picasso's women ragged collection
of parts
stitched together with paint

If I Die, Blame the Movies

It's okay to hide behind that couch, the stopping power
of Polyester is unmatched. Oak table, plywood doors,
a Bible or flask, even goose-down pillows can perform
the bullet catch at close range from a revolver, derringer,
.44 Magnum, Walter PPK, Gatling gun, Winchester.

I can ground a plane with a handgun, out-pace
a 747, get thrown out the emergency door in a fight
and still land on my feet, parachute neat as a handkerchief.
It's reasonable to dispatch cars with flaming arrows
to leaky gas tanks, to blow up sharks with oxygen tanks.

I can trust mysterious strangers and men in white hats,
nuns, mothers, and young lovers, but never a man in black,
never a brown man with a leather duster, eye-patch, turban,
handlebar mustache, shifty eyes. Never what is foreign,
unknown. Strange. This is everything we know of life.

The Girl Who Drew Lines on her Skin

Everyone's inked these days. No risk, no rebellion
when Sadie's mother's got a tramp stamp.

The girl razors new veins like a grid, treasure
mapped with exes and ohs. The game can't be won.
She's a ritual sacrifice, cutting to exorcise what isn't
in the blood. Her monster lives mine-deep,
can't be coaxed through thin wrists
as a trickle-down rivulet, gas-leak slow.
She's learned to flay layers, never
touching the core. Sever every nerve.
Leave nothing that can scar.

The Superman Poems

Hands

Before he knew hands could
splinter bone like birch,
he held birds, small enough
to squeeze, black eyes
buttons popping.

Every boy has a place for treasure:
gold-veined rocks, pennies flattened
shiny beneath the 5:00 from Granville,
lucky rabbit's foot, sleek crow's feather.
A robin.

Strength

Prays over small wings, kittens,
new chicks lowered into cold ground,
tenderness and failure.

Ma and Pa know only
the secrets he brings home, soft hands
he washes before supper.

Last Son

Did you not
understand
he was last?

Only.

Dead world
made manifest
made man.

Last son
of a dead sun
crimson fire, cobalt sky.

Memories freight
his bones (history, geography).
Rivers ripple, veins
in white-ice. Muscles
shift, tectonic
plates of a new world.

Family crest sears
his flesh blazes, brands
his chest.

Krypton

All knowledge
of home stored
in his cells, base code
a double helix read
in blood.

After him:
nothing —
emptiness,
minor correction
on star charts.

Zod

Others come. Criminals.
Refugees. Sent away.
The worst
preserved, specimens.

He is: His father,
mother, council,
an entire people. Judge,
executioner,
light spiralling

out,
falling
rock.

He is body,
brain, blink.

Heart, a burning
sun.

Kryptonite *

Superman is nowhere to be seen.

Lex Luthor rattles bars, creates a complex
machine, amalgam of fluorescent fixtures,
paperclips, a ballpoint pen. Escapes.

A figure in a winter-white parka with
fur-rimmed hood, bald head bare as Krypton,
drives nuclear power skiis across Serbian fields.

He will cross all lines for this:
sodium lithium boron silicate hydroxide

inventory of commonalities,
rock dragged inertial through space
behind the ship,
minerals irradiated and blown,
to seed other planets
so somewhere
a piece of home lives on.

Phone Booths

He dreams escape.

Clear glass cage diffusing light,
fingerprints, noseprints,
a stuck-gum tongue.

He shouldn't notice but Super-Speed

　　　　means the rest of the world

　　　　slows

everything turns relief, detail, infinitesimal

　　　　movement: air-slap of pigeon wings

　　　　newspaper peeled back, onion-thin

　　　　sound, heels grinding.

From above
he notes dead zones, dark cysts on an x-ray.
Witness to all, city laid out skeletal before him —
every artery, joint, capillary he could eradicate, make right
with a surgical strike. Luthor is right
to be afraid.

The Water Trick

He could drown here, weld edges
shut with heated glares, burst the water main six feet
below surface concrete. He sees it all: copper pipe

twisting, all bends and angles, earthworm-silent
under the city, alive. Water rushing upward
against the natural order.

His steel frame like the bones of a skyscraper.
He can hold his breath forever,
or long enough people would notice.

In this aquarium for one, sea-blue,
he's lobster-red, an easy catch.

Expanding Outward

His personal big bang
explodes inside out —
space no longer delineated by glass walls,
clothes shed like leper's skin,
Clark Kent discarded, dead weight.

Some days he tears up.

The ill-fitting brown suit hangs in beef jerky
strips, cheap cotton peels away revealing
blue, red, the truth of his body.

Clark Kent? Glasses thick-rimmed and useless. He can grind his own
from sand. The Metropolis Yellow Pages, ink-smudged, ripple
in a sudden unexplained wind. No one notices.

He misses the pinwheel clatter of cards he fastened
to his spokes, the ones that measured every mile he tried to fly
from Kansas dust and farm-heavy ache to a world
he could never call home.

Serpents

In his true form
the "S" sun-red, serpenting
across his chest,

he waits for heat to roust
his blood under this sun,
yellow and foreign.

Enclosed Spaces

He's tried elevators, bathroom stalls, broom closets.

He has his favourites. Corner of 12th and Vine. More elbow-room and three walls covered by ads.

Clean

Chlorine and powdered soap, baking soda like his mother used to scrub the farmhouse floor, brush brittle as old china. He tries scouring, sweeping, pushing and scraping, but this is a dying planet, ice-white and frothed with water. He cannot wipe the slate.

* Recently, a mineral matching the chemical composition of the fictional substance "kryptonite" was found in Serbia. It will likely be called Jadarite, after the region where it was discovered.

Girls Named Paula

> "I haven't seen Fonzie this upset since Paula Petralunga became a nun." —*Happy Days*

Hollywood showgirls with falsies and lopsided teens with
with overlarge brains, crammed tight as a locker. She's
brace-face and glasses, virginity sealed between mass
and confession. The right time, the wrong girl, more issues
than Ms., alphabetical lists, righteousness clamped in an uptight
fist. Side-kicked to the curb, she's the BFF, back stab, the frump
who got dumped, the girl all used up. She's yesterday's blues,
gift with purchase, sidecar, third wheel, first to lose her head
at slasher summer camp. Or forty, mouse brown, more ash on top
than Mt. St. Helen's, she's past prime time. Somebody's secretary,
mother, ex-wife, victim of mugger, a snore. She's a secret panel,
broken bottle bar fight, swims with sharks. Garter stitch, tramp
stamp, paper-cut sharp. She's sensible shoes in navy and orange,
solid oak table, a mirror, a torrent, a knife in the drawer. She's
corsets unlaced and rum-soaked cigars, a good bra, a raincoat.
Pink edge of a scar.

Acknowledgements

It takes a village to bring a book to publication. I can't possibly name everyone who has helped me along this path, but if you're reading this, you're one of them. Thank you.

Sincere thanks to Michael Kenyon, editor, who was a joy to work with. Like an archaeologist, he gently brushed aside the extraneous bits to reveal the essential artifacts underneath, and I am grateful. Thanks to Thistledown Press for this opportunity, and to the spirit of John V. Hicks who showed me that poets lived where I lived.

I'm grateful to previous editors and mentors that I've worked with during this journey, particularly Sylvia Legris, Susan Musgrave, and Karen Solie. Thanks to UBC's MFA Optional Residency program, Sage Hill Writing Experience, St. Peter's Abbey and St. Michael's retreat centre, and for the support of the Saskatchewan Writers' Guild through many years of membership and community. Thanks also to the editors of the following journals who published many of these poems for the first time in slightly different versions: *Grain, CV2*, *Room*, *Prairie Fire*, *Spring, The Fieldstone Review*, *The New Quarterly*, *On Spec*.

This book is dedicated to my parents, Jane and Allan Isinger, and my grandparents, Fred and Evelyn Russell, who read me poems. To my brother, who gave me better books. To my dear friend Susan who passed away when we were thirty-one, and to her sister Alice, who became the sister I never had. To my closest friends: Coline, Craig, Nicole, Nikoline, Isabelle. To my writing groups: Saskatchewan Children's Writers Round Robin and the D'lish group.

Last but not least, my grateful heart belongs to one person, my husband, Trent. Thank you for believing in me. Forever and for always.